World of Design

Festival Decorations

Anne Civardi

Photography by Sam Hare & Jane Paszkiewicz

SEA-TO-SEA

Mankato Collingwood London

This edition first published in 2010 by
Sea-to-Sea Publications
Distributed by Black Rabbit Books
P.O. Box 3263
Mankato, Minnesota 56002

Library of Congress Cataloging-in-Publication Data

Civardi, Anne.
  Festival decorations / Anne Civardi ; photography by Sam Hare &
Jane Paszkiewicz.
     p. cm. -- (World of design)
  Includes bibliographical references and index.
  ISBN 978-1-59771-208-8 (hardcover : alk. paper)
  1. Holiday decorations--Juvenile literature. 2. Handicraft--Juvenile
literature. I. Hare, Sam. II. Paszkiewicz, Jane. III. Title.
  TT900.H6C59 2010
  745.594'1--dc22
                                           2008043071

  9 8 7 6 5 4 3 2

Published by arrangement with the Watts Publishing
Group Ltd., London.

Design: Rachel Hamdi and Holly Fulbrook
Editor: Ruth Thomson

The author would like to thank the following people
for the loan of items from their collection:
Shefjan Designs (www.shefjandesigns.com): rangoli, 4, 23;
mehendi, 23. Casa Mexicana (www.casamexicanafolkart.com):
Tree of Life,15; Mexicolore (www.mexicolore.co.uk): butterfly, 2;
flags, 4; skull and coffin, 10; Eye of God, 18; feather headdress, 27.
Elaine Lindsay (www.somethingcorny.co.uk): corn dollies, 22.
Beata and Glenn (www.polcraft.co.uk): Polish paper-cuts, 4, 7.
The Patterson Creek Company (www.wreaths-unlimited.com):
wreaths, 2, 22. Barbie Cambell Cole (barbiecc@mail.com): headdresses, 4, 26. The Great Little Trading Co. (www.gltc.co.uk):
gingerbread house, 10. Viva La Frida (www.vivalafrida.co.uk):
Tree of Life, 4. Silly Jokes, Joke and Party Shop (www.sillyjokes.co.uk):
paper dragon, 5; piñata, 6. Brize Norton Primary School: harvest
loaf, 5; Islington Education Library Service (www.objectlessons.org):
fans, 1, 2; skull, 4; Christmas balls, 5; card, 5; paper cut-out, 5, 7;
corn dolly, 5; Evil Eye, 5; lion head, 6; lantern, 14; menorah, 11;
money packets, 19; headdress, 27.
Special thanks to Diana Marsh for her help and advice.

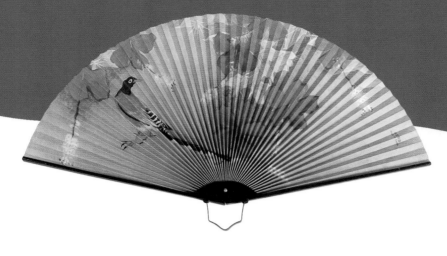

Contents

Paper-cut flags from Mexico

Chinese New Year paper lantern

Papier-mâché "Day of the Dead" skull from Mexico

Polish Easter paper-cut

Different decorations

Throughout the year, people everywhere create amazing, colorful, and unusual decorations to use at festivals and celebrations.

They decorate their homes, streets, cities, and schools to celebrate birthdays, weddings, religious festivals, and carnivals. Some people decorate the graves of their dead relatives.

Mexican Tree of Life candlestick

Festive Kuba mask from Africa

Fur hat worn at festivals by Tibetan men

4

Hand-painted card to celebrate the festival of Diwali in India

Glass Evil Eye (nazarlik) from Turkey

Chinese dragon paper-cut

At festivals, people hold big feasts, fly flags, and wear exotic costumes and masks, as they sing and dance in long parades.

This book tells you about all kinds of festive decorations, made from paper, wood, corn, chocolate, feathers, and even human hair. It shows you how to make some of your own, using decorations from all over the world as inspiration.

Loaf of bread in the shape of a wheat sheaf to celebrate an English Harvest Festival

Corn dolly from Scotland

Decorative paper fan from Japan

Chinese New Year paper dragon

5

Paper decorations

For more than 2,000 years, people have made exotic paper decorations to celebrate special days, such as Chinese New Year, Easter, and the Day of the Dead in Mexico.

To celebrate their New Year, Chinese people wear lion-head masks made from bamboo covered with papier-mâché. The eyes and tongue are on wire and wobble when the wearer moves.

In Mexico, piñatas, filled with candy and toys, are a traditional birthday party game. Children wearing blindfolds take turns hitting the piñata with a stick until it smashes open and the candy tumbles out.

Look closer

- Papier-mâché has been molded into a donkey shape to make this piñata.
- It has been covered with strips of tissue paper cut to create colorful fringes.

- The design of this paper-cut is symmetrical, which means it is exactly the same on both sides. It was created by folding a circle of blue paper in half before it was cut.
- Small pieces of colored paper were glued on top.

☼ *At Easter in Poland, people decorate their houses with paper-cuts. A Polish woman made this one using sheep-shearing scissors, without any drawing.*

Look closer

- The butterfly below was cut with scissors from a piece of soft tissue paper. Parts were dyed after it was cut.

☼ *In November, Mexicans celebrate the Day of the Dead when they remember their dead relatives. People make papier-mâché skeletons to honor the dead. This skull is filled with dried beans and is used as a rattle.*

☼ *The Chinese are skilled paper-cutters. During festivals, they decorate their doors and windows with delicate paper-cuts that often reflect the life of the people who made them. Paper-cuts are also called "window flowers."*

Making a paper piñata

1 Blow up a large balloon. Balance it on a bowl and cover it with papier-mâché (see page 30). Leave it to dry.

- a large balloon • a bowl
- newspaper • magazine pages
- white glue and water • party treats
- thin cardboard • adhesive tape
- tissue paper • scissors
- a glue pen • string or wire

2 Pop the balloon and cut a hole in the top of the paper ball. Fill the ball with candy and party treats.

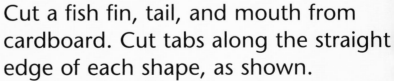

3 Add more papier-mâché to cover the hole.

4 Cut a fish fin, tail, and mouth from cardboard. Cut tabs along the straight edge of each shape, as shown.

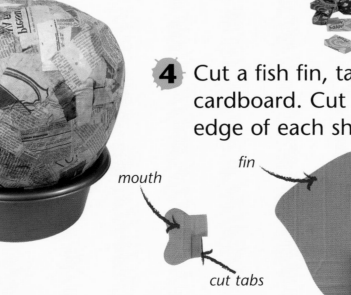

mouth

fin

tail

cut tabs

cut tabs

4 Bend the tabs. Tape the fin, tail, and mouth to the papier-mâché ball to create a fish.

5 Cover the cardboard pieces with papier-mâché so they are firmly attached to the ball. Let it dry.

6 Fold long strips of different colors of tissue paper in half. Cut snips along the open edges. Glue the strips all over the fish.

Make a hole in the fin.

7 Thread wire or string through a hole in the top of the fish's fin. Hang up your piñata and let the party begin!

Celebrating with food

Food plays an important part at festivals and celebrations. People may spend many days preparing traditional feasts for their family and friends.

☼ At Christmas, people in North America and Europe make gingerbread houses to decorate their tables. Gingerbread has been baked for more than 1,000 years.

Look closer

- Six pieces of baked gingerbread were joined together with icing to form the walls and roof of the house.

- It was decorated with piped icing and candies.

☼ On the Day of the Dead, Mexicans leave offerings of food, such as this sugar skull and sugar coffin, to the dead.

Look closer

- The skeleton in the sugar coffin (right) sits up when the red string is pulled.

Easter eggs are an important part of the Easter tradition. They are a symbol of Spring and new life. For Christians, Easter eggs represent the rebirth of Christ.

- Before these real eggs were decorated, the yolks and whites were removed. A craftswoman made a small hole at each end. She blew into one hole, forcing the contents of the egg out of the other.

- She carefully hand-painted the thin, delicate shells.

Look closer

- The "Tray of Togetherness" (below) has different compartments, each filled with a different symbolic food. Peanuts, for example, represent a long and healthy life; lychee nuts represent close family relationships; red melon seeds mean happiness and joy.

During Chinese New Year, people offer guests a box filled with nuts and sweet things. This is known as the "Tray of Togetherness" or chyuhn haap.

11

Gingerbread people

You will need adult help with this project.

You will need

- gingerbread dough (see page 31)
- a rolling pin and board • a gingerbread cookie cutter • a cookie sheet • raisins • silver balls • an icing bag • icing

1 Ask an adult to preheat the oven to 350°F (180°C). Roll the gingerbread dough (see page 31 for the recipe) on a lightly floured surface until it is about ⅛in (3mm) thick.

2 Use a cutter to cut out gingerbread people.

3 Put the cookies on a lightly greased cookie sheet. Decorate them with raisins or silver balls for the eyes, a nose, or buttons.

4 Ask an adult to put them in the oven. Bake them for 10–12 minutes, or until they feel firm when lightly pressed with a fingertip.

5 When the gingerbread people are cool, decorate them with piped icing.

icing

Tip: Gingerbread people make great Christmas gifts and decorations. You can poke a hole in the figures' heads before they are baked. Thread ribbon through the holes and hang them on your Christmas tree.

Festivals of light

All over the world, people of many different religions light candles or lanterns to celebrate important events. These festivals are known as "Festivals of Light."

Look closer

- The lamps below are made from clay that has been fired (baked hard).
- Candlelight glows through holes that were poked into the clay when it was still wet and soft.
- Both lamps are decorated with pearly paint to make them gleam.

Hanukkah, the Jewish Festival of Lights, lasts for eight days. Each evening, families place one candle in the menorah, a nine-branched candlestick, like this, and light it with a special blessing. The middle candle (shamash or "servant") is used to light all the others.

In November, Hindus celebrate their New Year with a Festival of Lights, known as Diwali. To welcome Lakshmi, the goddess of wealth, they place little lamps, called "divas," in their windows and doorways.

For more than 100 years, craftspeople in Metepec, Mexico, have made colorful clay sculptures in the shape of trees, called "Trees of Life." At Christmas, Mexicans decorate their homes with nativity "Trees of Life."

Look closer

- The nativity scene shows clay figures of Joseph and Mary, baby Jesus, the Archangel Gabriel, as well as shepherds and animals, in a stable.

- Above them is a figure of God with outstretched arms.

- All around are painted clay flowers, birds, and angels.

This decoration is called a Christingle, which means "Christ-light." On Christmas Eve, at candlelit services in England, children each hold a Christingle.

Look closer

Each part of a Christingle has a special meaning.

- The orange stands for the world.

- The red ribbon represents Jesus' blood, when He died on the cross.

- The sticks represent the four seasons.

- The candle stands for the light of the world.

- The candies remind Christians of the food God gives them.

Making a Diwali lamp

1 Roll some clay into a small ball. Press your thumb into the center to make a hollow.

- self-hardening clay
- a board • a nightlight
- a fork • a paintbrush
- acrylic paints

Press thumb into clay.

2 Carefully mold the clay into a little bowl, making sure a nightlight can fit in. Put the nightlight in the bowl.

nightlight

3 Use your forefinger and thumb to pinch in the sides of the bowl. Press a pattern into the top with a fork.

4 Use the end of
a paintbrush to poke
holes through the clay.
Leave it to dry.

 5 Paint your lamp
inside and out with
rich-looking colors.

6 Paint patterns on the
outside of the lamp.

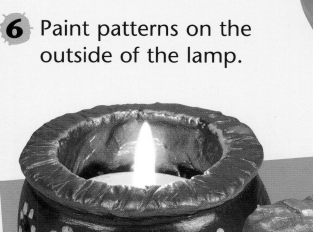

*Tip: You can make
Diwali lamps in all
shapes and sizes.*

Good luck greetings

There are many special occasions and celebrations when people give their friends or family presents that they hope will give protection and bring good luck.

The Huichol Indians of Mexico weave brightly colored "Ojo de Dios" (Eye of God) decorations to watch over babies and give them good luck when they are born.

Look closer

- Thread or yarn is woven around two crossed sticks.

- The white diamond shape (central "eye") is woven by the child's father when it is born.

- Each different colored "eye" is added every year until the child reaches five.

Chinese people put a lucky cat, like this, in their homes and work places. They believe that a lucky cat with its left paw raised will protect them and give them good fortune.

In India, a coconut, which is a symbol of good luck and wealth, is often presented to a bride and groom on their wedding day. Indians hope that the life of a married couple is like a coconut—full of sweetness, even in difficult times.

☼ *Some wedding coconuts in India are very fancy. This one is wrapped in shiny gold ribbon and decorated with beads.*

☼ *In the past, Japanese Kokeshi dolls were given as gifts to celebrate a child's birth or to remember one who had died. Farmers thought they would bring a successful harvest if their children played with them.*

Look closer

- The wooden dolls have a round or cylindrical body.
- Some have separate heads that nod, others are made from a single piece of wood.
- They are all hand-painted and no two are alike.

At Chinese New Year, children receive little red and gold packets containing money, known as "lucky money." The Chinese believe that red and gold are lucky colors.

Making an Eye of God

Back

Front

5in (13cm)

11in (28cm)

two thin sticks ● embroidery
thread or thin yarn in six different
colors ● a pencil ● scissors

1 Tie two thin sticks together with
embroidery thread, making an X,
as shown. Do not cut off the thread.

2 Number the sticks from 1 to 4, as shown.
Bring the thread to the front between
sticks 3 and 4. Pull it over sticks 3 and 2.
Wrap it behind stick 2 and
bring it to the front again
between sticks 2 and 3. Pull it over
sticks 2 and 1. Wrap it behind stick 1.

3 Pull the thread over sticks
1 and 4. Wrap it behind
stick 4 and then stick 3.
This is one complete
round. Wrap more
rounds in the same way
until you have made a
central "eye" in one color.

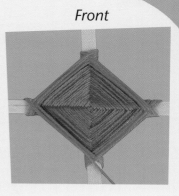

4 Tie on another color, making sure the knot is at the back. Continue to weave as before.

5 Carry on weaving until you have used all six colors and are about 1in (2cm) from the ends of sticks 2, 3, and 4. Do not cut the final thread.

6 Wrap the final thread and one other color around the handle. Knot the ends.

7 Add tassels (see page 31) onto the ends of sticks 2, 3, and 4.

Decorations from nature

At celebrations all over the world, people decorate their homes with things made from natural materials. Some people even decorate themselves.

Look closer

- The skirt of the corn dolly on the left is made from wheat stalks.

- Her arms were created by braiding wheat stalks.

  - Wheat stalks have been twisted into a spiral shape to create the corn dolly on the right.

☀ *At festivals, such as Diwali and weddings, Indian women create* rangolis, *like this one made from rice powder, turmeric, and stone powder. They make them close to the entrance of their homes as an invitation to Laxmi, the goddess of knowledge and wealth.*

Look closer

- The symmetrical design of this vibrant pink, green, blue, and white rangoli is made up of circles and symbols. Circles enclose the central pattern to stop evil from entering the colorful world.

Henna painting (*mehendi*) is important to Indian brides. Before her wedding, a bride has her hands and feet decorated to show the strength of love in her marriage. She believes that the darker the mehendi, the more her husband will love her.

☀ *It took more than four hours to paint this bride's hands and feet. The patterns were painted with a paste made from henna, eucalyptus oil, lemon juice, and tea. Henna is made from the leaves of the henna plant.*

Making a corn dolly

1 Fold a bundle of raffia, about 18in (44cm) long, in half. Tightly wrap a length of raffia near the top of the bundle to make a head and a neck.

2 Cut another bundle of raffia, about 5in (12cm) long, for the arms. Push it through the middl of the body and tie it just below the arms to make a waist.

3 Wrap raffia around the arms and chest, like this.

4 For the hair, make a long raffia braid. Fold the braid in half and tie the ends.

5 Tie the braided hair to the top of the dolly's head.

6 For the hat, make a ring of raffia to fit the dolly's head. Wrap raffia around and around the ring.

7 Put the hat on the dolly's head. Decorate her with dried grasses, dried flowers, and ribbon.

25

Festive headdresses

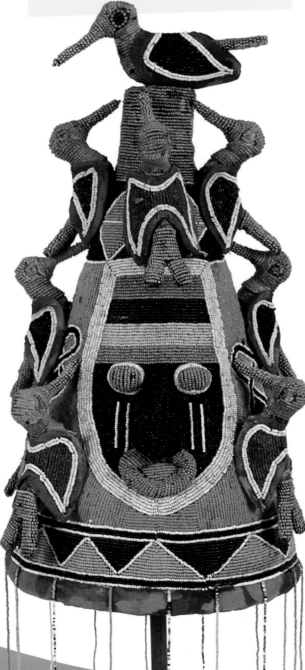

In the past, the king of the Yoruba tribe, in Africa, wore a beaded crown, like this, at public ceremonies. The beaded veil hid his face from his people, who were not allowed to look directly at him.

Headdresses made of feathers, beads or wood may be worn at religious ceremonies or to celebrate a good harvest or past victories in battle.

Look closer

- Beaded birds surround a beaded face that represents the king. The birds represent women, showing that the king cannot rule without their support.

- There is a bird on the top, which is believed to hold medicines that protect the king.

This Chinese Yao Shaman's hat is made from human hair. A shaman is thought to have powers that protect people from evil and disease.

- The bright, contrasting colors of this feather headdress create a symmetrical design.

Every July, men and boys in Oaxaca, Mexico, perform the Feather Dance, wearing huge, heavy tin and feather headdresses.

At festivals in Zimbabwe, Shona men wear headdresses made from ostrich feathers attached to a beaded headband.

Headdresses, like this, are worn at harvest festivals by the Bambara tribe of Mali.

The wooden animal on top of the headdress (left) represents a mythical antelope, called the Chi Wara. The Bambara believed that it taught their people how to farm, showing them how to find seeds and dig holes with its extra long antlers.

Making a bird headdress

- a large sheet of poster paper
- smaller sheets in different colors
- adhesive tape ● scissors ● glue
- a small cardboard tube

1 Wrap the sheet of poster paper into a cone large enough to fit your head. Tape it at the back.

tape

2 Cut off the top and bottom of the cone.

3 Cut two strips of colored paper, long enough to fit around the base of the cone.

4 Cut a paper bird shape with a tab. Glue an eye and a wing onto each side. Make six birds.

Cut a zigzag pattern along one strip. Glue this on top of the other strip. Glue both around the bottom of the cone hat.

tab

28

5 Cut an oval face shape. Glue on strips of paper to make a hat.

6 Draw a nose, eyes, and a ring on a small cardboard tube. Cut out the shape. Paint it or glue on colored paper, as shown.

7 Bend in the sides of the nose and glue it on to the face.

8 Glue the face onto the front of the hat. Bend the tabs and glue two birds to each side of the hat and one in the front. Cut a slit in the hole at the top of the hat and slot the sixth bird into it.

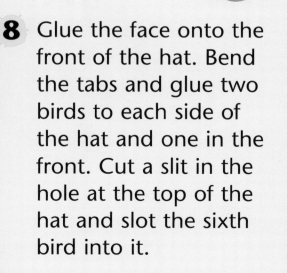

29

Handy hints

Making papier-mâché

1 Tear newspaper into small pieces and put them into a pile. Tear pages from a color magazine into similar pieces. Keep these in a separate pile.

newspaper pieces

magazine pieces

2 Mix white glue with the same amount of water in a bowl or pitcher.

3 Dip the newspaper pieces into the glue mixture and overlap them all over the balloon, starting at the knot.

4 Once the balloon is covered with a layer of newspaper pieces, cover it with a layer of magazine pieces. Alternate layers of newspaper and magazine pieces until you have made five layers altogether.

Remember: it can take several days for papier-mâché to dry completely and become hard.

Making gingerbread dough

Ingredients

scant ½ cup soft brown sugar; 2 tbsp corn syrup;
1 tbsp molasses; 1 tsp cinnamon; 1 tsp ginger;
a pinch of ground cloves;
grated rind of half an orange; ⅓ cup butter;
½ tsp baking soda; 1¾ cups all-purpose flour.

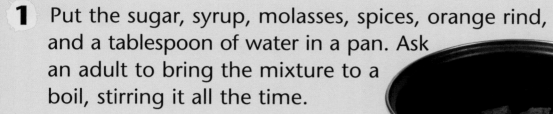

1 Put the sugar, syrup, molasses, spices, orange rind, and a tablespoon of water in a pan. Ask an adult to bring the mixture to a boil, stirring it all the time.

2 Remove the pan from the heat and stir in the butter, cut into small lumps. Add the baking soda. Stir in the flour gradually until you have a smooth dough. Leave it to cool for 30 minutes.

Making a tassel

1 Wrap thread around a small piece of cardboard.

2 Slide it off gently. Bend it in half and hold it against the end of the stick. Wind thread around the stick, and the bottom of the tassel.

3 Cut through the loops.

31

Glossary

festival celebration of an important event or day, often based on religion or tradition

harvest the time when people gather in their crops of food

offering something, such as food, given at a festival or celebration

spirit a supernatural being

symbol something that stands for or represents something else, especially an object that represents something abstract

traditional beliefs or customs that are handed down from one generation to the next

Index